JUL 2013

W9-BAJ-748

our wonderful
weather

valerie bodden

thunderstorms

creative education

our wonderful
weather

Published by Creative Education
P.O. Box 227, Mankato, Minnesota 56002
Creative Education is an imprint of The Creative Company
www.thecreativecompany.us

Design and production by Christine Vanderbeek
Art direction by Rita Marshall
Printed by Corporate Graphics in the United States of America

Photographs by Alamy (J Marshall-Tribaleye Images, Stock Italia), Corbis (Bettmann, Warren Faidley, Mike Hollingshead/Science Faction, Jim Reed Photography, Eric Nguyen), Dreamstime (Greg Blomberg, Patty Jenks, Christy Thompson, Marek Uliasz, Chris White), Getty Images (Justin Bane/US Navy, Johner, Joe Raedle, Erik Simonsen, Steve Taylor), iStockphoto (Cshoeps, Steve Geer, Image Source, MvH, Jane Norton, Yahor Piaskouski, Charles Schug, Clint Spencer, VM)

Library of Congress Cataloging-in-Publication Data

Bodden, Valerie.
Thunderstorms / by Valerie Bodden.
Summary: A simple exploration of thunderstorms, examining how these warm-weather storms
develop, the relationship between lightning and thunder, and the damage thunderstorms can cause.
Includes bibliographical references and index.
ISBN 978-1-60818-149-0
1. Thunderstorms—Juvenile literature. I. Title.
QC968.2.B63 2012
551.55'4—dc22   2010052764

CPSIA: 082912 PO1605

2 4 6 8 9 7 5 3

contents

A thunderstorm is a storm with thunder and lightning. Thunderstorms form when warm air and water vapor rise into the sky. As the water vapor rises, it gets colder and turns into water drops that form clouds.

The water in storm clouds makes them look thick and gray

Sometimes the clouds grow very tall, with a flat top. These are called cumulonimbus (KYOO-myoo-loh-NIM-bus) clouds. They are thunderstorm clouds. Wind pushes them across the sky.

A cumulonimbus cloud can be 10 miles (16 km) high

During a thunderstorm, rain pours down, and winds whip. Lightning flashes, and thunder booms. Lightning is a bolt of electricity.

Thunder is the sound lightning makes. You hear thunder after you see lightning because sound does not travel as fast as light.

There are many kinds of thunderstorms. Single-cell thunderstorms usually last only about half an hour.

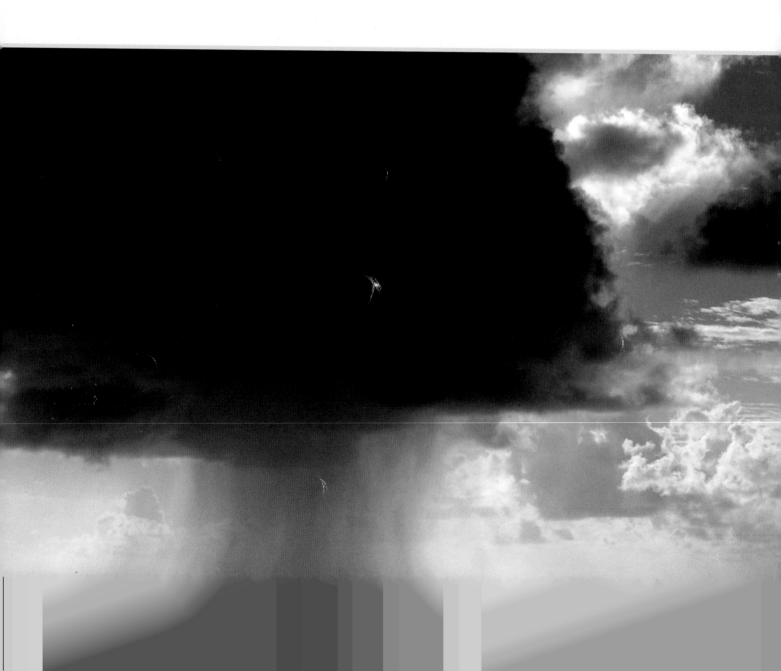

Supercell thunderstorms are very strong. They can make hail, strong downward winds called downbursts, and tornadoes.

supercell thunderstorm

Any type of thunderstorm can be a severe storm. Severe storms have hail the size of a quarter or bigger. Their winds blow at 58 miles (93 km) per hour or faster.

Severe thunderstorms can be dangerous to houses and other buildings

In July 1976, a thunderstorm over the Rocky Mountains flooded the Big Thompson River in Colorado. The rushing water killed 139 people. In May 1995, a strong thunderstorm in Dallas, Texas, produced tornadoes, floods, and hail as big as softballs!

Heavy rain in the Big Thompson River caused this 1976 flood

Thunderstorms can cause other problems, too. If lightning strikes a tree, it can start a wildfire. If lightning strikes people,

it can hurt or kill them. Hail can damage cars and kill plants.

High winds and tornadoes can knock down trees and buildings.

hail

During the summer, thunderstorms form in many places. If you see lightning or hear thunder, get inside! Stay inside until there is no thunder for 30 minutes. Then you can peek out to see if the storm has left a rainbow behind!

RISING AND FALLING

Thunderstorms form when warm, moist air rises above cooler air. To see how warm temperatures rise above cold temperatures, first make a blue ice cube by freezing water mixed with blue food coloring. Drop the ice cube into one end of a clear plastic food container (about the size of a shoe box) filled with warm water. Add three drops of red food coloring to the other end of the container. Watch what happens!

GLOSSARY

flooded — overflowed the banks of a river or lake so that large amounts of water covered land that was usually dry

forecast — to try to figure out what is going to happen in the future, such as during the next day or week

hail — small balls of ice that sometimes fall from clouds during thunderstorms

radar — a system that uses radio waves and computers to measure how far away something (such as a cloud or thunderstorm) is and how fast it is moving

satellites — machines that circle Earth in space; weather satellites can take pictures of clouds and measure temperatures

water vapor — water that has turned into drops so tiny that it rises into the air and becomes invisible

READ MORE

Harris, Caroline. *Science Kids: Weather*. London: Kingfisher, 2009.

Mezzanotte, Jim. *Thunderstorms*. Pleasantville, N.Y.: Weekly Reader Early Learning Library, 2010.

WEB SITES

FEMA for Kids: Thunderstorms

http://www.fema.gov/kids/thunder.htm
Learn more about how to stay safe during a thunderstorm.

National Geographic Kids: Lightning Photos

http://kids.nationalgeographic.com/kids/photos/gallery/lightning/
Check out some amazing pictures of lightning.

INDEX